DAIRY OF A Crewmates year on a Spaceship.

(An Among Us Unofficial Novel)

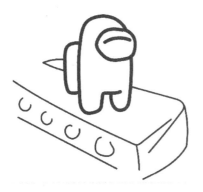

Part 1

Introduction

Fall, Day 1

Dear ~~Diary~~ (scratch that) Survival book. I am on a massive spaceship; I should have a cool title for these adventures of mine! Yes, you guessed it correctly, I am a crewmate. We are travelling to a recently discovered planet, it is called **'Aurelion'**.

AURELION

It is a planet full of gold, the scientists on the news promised it to be. I love shiny things, so I signed up for the exploration "hehe!".

Imagine all the snacks I can buy once I return.

Can't wait to see it!

Fall, Day 2

I forgot my favorite toy at home, I call him Beebo, it is a toy teddy that I always take with me.

beebo

I am bringing up Beebo because he helps me walk to the bathroom once it is dark and it is dark right now and I really need to pee.

Flammable objects are banned in space, they thought we would burn everything down. Good thing I snuck some candles from home anyway, who would've thought I'd need them. They laughed at my idea for sneaking candles with me to the ship. Look who is laughing now! Ha, I am so smart! ...   I still don't have my teddy... Please fix the lights I need to pee! Help!

Fall, Day 3

I was thinking back about yesterday's events... the ship stopped because of sudden electricity issues; everything was running smoothly so it is making me suspicious. How could this happen and why. I have been thinking for hours now, how this could happen, they even duct tapped the switches, so they stay on. It is suspicious... I feel like I could figure out how this happened and who did this.

That's it! I am going on a mission! I will infiltrate the others, find the prankster who turned off lights and find my revenge for not letting me to go the toilet. The game is on! Just you watch you... prankster... Hmm... I feel like there could be a better word for this. Infiltrator? No... Mastermind? Also no... Something catchy and cool to be my ultimate nemesis! IMPOSTOR!

space Impostor

Fall, Day 6

I have been conducting my secret investigation for the

last 3 days, there are 10 of us here. I am sure I counted correctly, I have been having troubles counting because everyone is always moving and running around the ship, but I am sure I am right.

To help me with my mission I have decided to find a partner. I have three candidates. First is Green, he is kind of slow at times and sometimes gets angry at the card task and slams the table, but he is nice.

me and friends with icecream

He gave me Ice cream. He can't be bad. If you must

know, I like people that bring me snacks.

Second candidate is White, she is wearing a white spacesuit with a rose emblem attached to her chest and a majestic hat.

Hmm I forgot about the third one... I just saw him in medbay, I wanted to have a chat with him but now he is gone... I was sure he walked in this room. It is like he disappeared into thin air. He

had a dark color suit…
suspicious.

Fall, Day 7

There haven't been any
interruptions lately and the
ship has been flying through
space without any hiccups. I
decided that I am going to
do my sample task today. It
takes time but it is
interesting to watch the
colors change. By the way I
decided that Green is going

to be my partner, he gave me cookies today.

COOKIE BOX

COOKIES

I chose Green because he is loyal, gives me snacks and all around a good guy if you ignore his snoring and how slow he is. I definitely did not choose Green because White said she is busy and does not have time for games and I didn't forget my third candidate. I am smart and cool! I should be the president of this ship.

Fall, Day 9

I knew I was right; I knew the Impostor exists. This is no game White. The fuel disappeared. This cannot be a coincidence. Green agrees with me, he said "Red, you the cool and calm collected president of this ship, are right". I might have added a word here and there, but you get the message.

I WAS RIGHT!

Fall, Day 10

I made a map of the entire ship to track everyone's location and the tasks they were doing.

Map guide

Engine

The engines are on the left side of the ship. Green and I were on the right side of the ship in the navigation room. I saw Pink and Orange hanging out together, so they were not close to the accident. I didn't see anyone else... I feel like I should call the meeting, but I only have one chance to do so. I must investigate. This is suspicious... Green agreed with me and said, "Yup the windows here sure are big".

green Looking wall

He is speaking in code to hide any suspicions. He sure is cool. I can't believe I didn't come up with that first.

Fall, Day 11

I have found my nemesis, no no, not the impostor, not yet that is. But another crewmate who is eyeing my president of the ship position. I was elected by Green and I as the leader of this ship, I sent invites to the other crewmates. It is not my fault they didn't show up. But now they are thinking about electing Dark blue as the leader, yes, he has a cool colored suit and a deep voice... Dark blue is the color I wanted but it was taken so I got red but that is beside the point.

crewmate on a pedestal as the leader

He doesn't even care about the impostor. He said those were some small technical issues and shouldn't worry about it. I raised my concerns about this, but I was ignored... Dark blue was elected as the leader and White wants to be the vice-leader. Look who is interested in games now Mrs. Busy.

Fall, Day 11

Late evening

I heard a knocking at my door... I was taking a light nap, so it startled me... The first thought that ran through my head was... is it the imposter... Was I too rash to tell everyone of my suspicions... Someone knocked again, this time louder.

knock at the door

I mustered up my spirits and went to take a look. You are not going to believe who It was. It was a ghost! No, I am joking it was one of the crewmates. 'Why would they visit me this late... oh no... some dark thoughts started running through my head but the figure in the dark stopped them with one sentence: "I believe in you Red" ... it slid an envelope below my door with a snack... How did it know I love chocolate? Envelopes can wait.

message

What a nice person, wait are my priorities wrong? Ah whatever, I will read the envelope tomorrow. Can't let this chocolate melt.

Fall, Day 12

After carefully inspecting the envelope, searching all over for a clue and after asking Green to taste it I have concluded it is a normal envelope. I displayed the content of the envelope in front of me. There were 2 pictures and a small note. The first was a picture of the switches.

switches with duct tape

There were 5 switches as there should be... why did he send me this picture? Green was starting to get bored in my room as all the snacks had been consumed and looked at the picture I was holding in my hand: "Huh, weird. Who uses duct tape on switches"? It finally hit me! Green, you are a genius. You felt I had reached a point of helplessness. Instead of solving it for me you showed me the way. The light in the dark for me. My sensei Green. Hmm... no. He is my assistant; he can't be my sensei... Now this is truly troublesome.

After pondering for a solid hour, I realized that I had gone off track. The switches. Someone had removed the duct tapes of the middle two switches and turned them off. It wasn't a coincidence. Someone is trying to stop us from reaching Aurelion. What is their reason for creating this chaos and who the hell duct tapes switches? AM IN A PRANK SHOW OR WHAT?

Fall, Day 16

Purple suggested we prepare for Halloween.

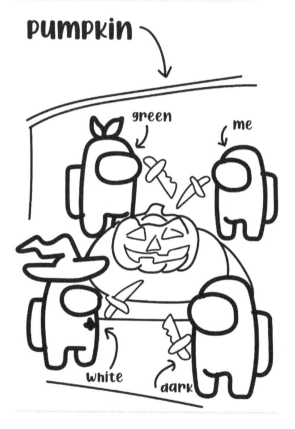

PUMPKIN

green

me

white

dark

Purple and his friend group Dark Green and Brown, said that he wants to have a fun activity to get to know each other better. Rest of the crewmates are excited about this idea. So, am I, surprisingly? Green and I have been brainstorming ideas for our costumes to go to the party. I told him that this is an important event for me as White will also be joining, she already said that she has a costume in mind that will shock all of us, so I want to be ready. Dark blue may have taken the president of the ship position from me, but he won't be able to take the coolest hat of the ship position from me. Watch your back Dark blue, I am coming for you!

Fall, Day 17

An alarming sound shook the entire ship. Red lights and loud beeping noises everywhere. This was a scary feeling. All of us together rushed towards the reactor only to find out it had been unplugged... Why would you make this much noise and bring everyone's attention towards the reactor... Oh no...? It clicked in my mind, the navigation

room. I ran as fast as I could,
If I am fast enough, they
might not have enough time
to leave. I can finally catch
my nemesis.

Running

THE IMPOSTOR!

I had never felt more lost in my life. No one was to be seen in the navigation room. I felt like I had him in the grasp of my palm. They just disappeared once they walked into the room. This is the second time this has happened to me. First my assistant candidate disappearing on me now the person in navigation room. Could there be a way for them to travel between the rooms without us crewmates knowing... but how...

Fall, Day 18

Emergency button

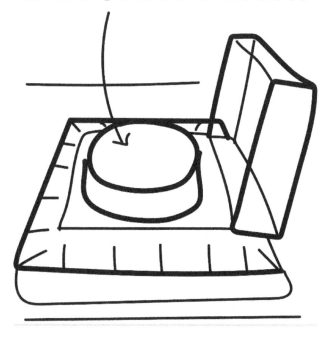

Dark blue decided to call a meeting and use his only button over this, what if you need to call everyone to tell them you ran out of snacks huh? What then Dark blue! *Scuff* This is our president, what a joke. Dark blue went on to explain that the Impostors had used the moment when everyone was busy getting ready for Halloween to strike. The Impostor had erased the coordinates to Aurelion. It is going to take us a few days to contact HQ to get the coordinates back, I can't believe no one wrote them down the first time. What a coincidence.

He asked who had been working at the cafeteria on the decorations and where were the others who hadn't been there at the moment.

crewmates

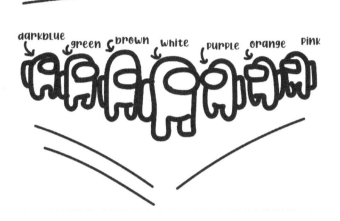

Oddly enough Dark blue, Dark green, Brown and White were all in the cafeteria. Usually, Purple is there with his friends too. Orange and Pink were together again, and they were in the admin room setting up the music for our Halloween event, they were looking for some spooky songs. Yellow said that he was busy, but no one can vouch for him which puts him in a bad position but yellow ran to the reactor once he heard the alarm. Then there is Purple. He is usually hanging out with his buddies Dark Green and Brown as I mentioned before but he was nowhere to be seen this time. He said he had to go to the toilet and had missed the panic. How do you miss those loud beeps and the horrible sound that comes with them? Even the lights change. That is truly suspicious Purple. I have my eyes on you and so does Green, I will just remind Green about it later. Right now, he is busy looking at the wall. He just can't help it.

After listening to everyone's whereabouts and

information they shared I told them that Green and I were together, and Dark blue called an end to this meeting. We have some new suspicions as of this meeting so I can't say Dark blue wasted his button. But I would be sad if I was Dark blue, imagine calling your button first. Sucks to be him. I can't wait to press mine!

Fall, Day 19

I returned to the scene of the crime. I recently examined the medbay station as well. I can't let go of the feeling that I am missing something obvious... something so simple that every kid in town knows about it. I stomped my foot in anger at my own cluelessness. Something rattled... Did I break something? Well, wouldn't be the first time now would It. I looked down and realized that I was standing on a vent... a vent... where have I seen... oh.

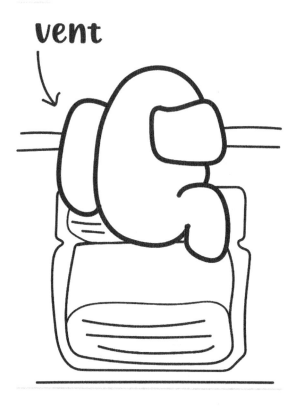

MEDBAY! MEDBAY HAS A VENT TOO!... Can the impostors use vents to hide and travel? That sounds absurd or does it. I am intrigued. I opened the vent to see if it led somewhere but I couldn't fit in. I saw something in the corner of my eye... a handkerchief.

Handkerchief

AHA, a clue Watson, a clue, hmm Green is not here. That is truly a shame, I have always wanted to do this. All is well. The only reason why it would be there was if someone had dropped it while using the vent. I have an idea. I need Green. No one and I am saying no one like their event preparations interrupted, **there will be consequences**. I heard that line in a movie, pretty cool right? I don't know what it means yet, but it sure does sound spooky.

Fall, Day 26

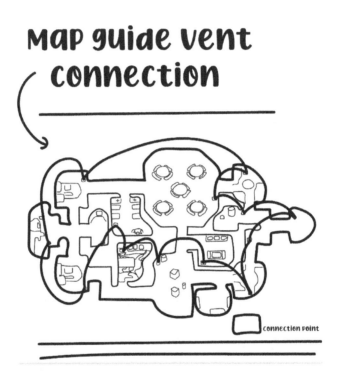

Map guide vent connection

connection point

Green and I have spent the entire last week figuring which vents connect and where do they go. I have figured out the system and drew it on my map. Both upper and the lower engine are connected to reactor. The security room is connected with medbay and the electric room. Cafeteria is connected with the admin room and the hallways of navigation. Navigation is connected with shields and weapons room. This is truly confusing I know. This will take me a few more days to remember but on the bright side we got a coffee machine. Yellow, found it in the storage. Coffee apparently helps you work I heard.

Fall, Day 29

I woke up in my comfy bed today. I was all snuggly and ready to have some hot chocolate, as usual the lights had been turned off. Damn Impostor, ruining my morning.. I didn't want to walk that much today, It is a long way to the switches.I couldn't make my morning hot chocolate without the electricity. I told you that Yellow found the coffee machine, It is a blessing and a curse.

coffee machine

It makes hot chocolate
which is the most amazing

drink on this ship and it also makes coffee. I hate the taste of coffee and the others who drink them go crazy. I honestly don't understand how does coffee work. It makes then run around and they can't do their tasks properly. The last time our ,recently established crews clown Brown had coffee, he spent 15min trying to shoot the asteroids down. It takes me 20 seconds. It is crazy.

Coffee is evil, mom was right.

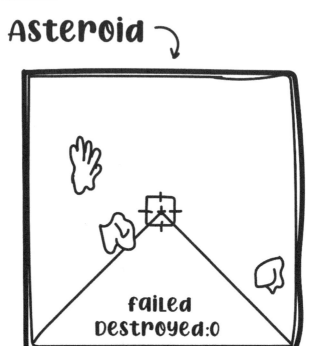

Fall, Day 30

It is one day till Halloween. It doesn't help that every month the 30th is the official garbage task day. Why are we worried about garbage a day before the mask ball? I HATE IT. It is not as bad as coffee, but how is this a thing. I don't want to spend the entire day doing garbage, I would rather listen to the radio and prepare my outfit to be the star of the show.

RADIO

Everyone will be wearing a mask and an outfit. No one will know who the other person is. Spooky and mysterious. Now that I think about it, this sounds like the perfect set up for an impostor.

Fall, Day 31

It is finally the day of event, I am so excited! IT IS HALLOWEEN! I have been preparing and waiting to show off my costume. Green apparently isn't interested in winning the costume contest so he will look for something else to do. Doesn't sound too convincing but I am not going to pay too much attention to it, I have got bigger fish to fry.

Wow! I walked into the cafeteria, all of the walls had been decorated. Some toy bats were hanging from the ceiling as well as a few carved pumpkins could be seen here and there.

I am going to enjoy this!

The party was going well, I greeted all of the attending crewmates and chatted a bit. It is hard to recognise each other with the masks but it is okay, it is not like we need to. The costume contest was starting soon and I was ready. This is my chance, my moment. My opportunity to leave a mark on this ship. This is it.

You may be suprised why I am this hyped, well it is because only 3 people signed up and I like my chances. I thought this would be a more popular contest. It is odd that White hasn't signed up.

WOOOHOO! The contest was under way, Dark blue was the host of the show, obviously with that voice of his. The first contestant was wearing a rubber duck on his head.. interesting choice of a hat. But that's good.

I can win. It was finally time to reveal my costume, my long awaited moment. BAM!

I walked out with confidence, I was shining.

Boom.. the alert went off... what.. no this is my moment...

It is a Halloween heist, someone attempted to steal the crewmates cards. They want to steal our card so we can't log in to the ship at the admin section.

id card

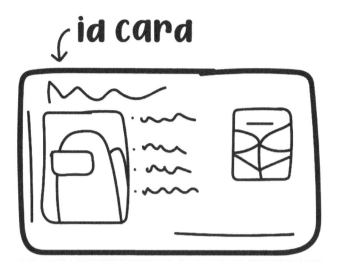

Everyone rushed to check their cards. We all left them at our rooms because of the costumes. The impostor is truly Among us.

There will be a thorough investigation in the following

days. Interestingly enough I never saw White today.

The theft attempt wasn't the biggest crisis today, the costume event was! It got cancelled and I didn't get to participate. They gave the award to the person with the duck on his head. What even is that! I just wanted to be included.. the winner got snacks and the coolest hat person award. Those snacks looked so crunchy..

How does Green win the best costume award.... What have I done to be punished this way, Green said he doesn't even care, I will smite you down Impostor, you made me run and you took my snacks. Bring it! I will catch you and you are going down.

Update: Green shared his snacks. I am less angry.

sharing

Fall, day 35

I can press the button to summon everyone for a meeting. I have done my research and made multiple investigations. I have Green

with me to have my back.
He hasn't betrayed my trust
before and he shall never do
so. My suspect is Purple.

Button)

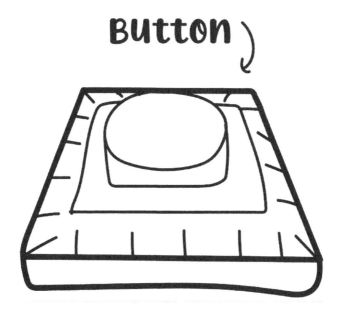

He was missing in the 2
latest emergencies. Once he
went to the toilet and said

he had missed all the alarms and what now and this time he didn't want to participate in the Halloween event. If that is not suspicious, I don't know what is.

I still haven't talked to Orange, he always stays quiet and only hangs out with Pink. The problem is that I had my eyes on Purple when the first emergency happened and I don't have evidence to prove my claims. What if there are two impostors.. a thought quickly crossed my mind but I ignored it. Too much thinking hurts my brain sometimes so let's stick with one.

Green came to my room with Orange. We were finally introduced, I know it is late but come on.

in Room

I was BUSY! They are brothers,Pink and Orange that is,so after the emergencies they knew they could only trust each other, but they also knew they needed help.So Orange came to me. It turns out Orange was the one who sent me the envelope, that was a passive way to help me out but now they thought this needed a more active approach. He came to inform me that they are thinking of organising a meeting and that they have been doing investigations.

papers

A list of suspects was made, Purpl,Brown,Dark green as well as White. I was suprised to hear Whites name come up but I agreed with the Purple pick. He seems suspicious in my eyes too. I informed them about the fact that impostors can use vents to travel which shocked Orange greatly but after taking his time they believed me. He said there could be another impostor and we should stay careful. He wants me to call the meeting and present everyone with the information. I was chosen as our representative. Wooo, I do love the attention. I was given some more snacks

which is cool. I feel like he is
buttering me up.. Hmm..

Evening struck.. I called the
meeting and started to tell
them the information we

had gathered. Some of the crew members started to frown after hearing what I had to say, some even shouted and said that I was making this up. Halloween is over they said, this is no time for pranks. I was getting scared, no one had my back, Green was missing, and the brothers were just keeping quiet and smiled. Why aren't they saying anything. I called out to them but nothing... Pink just looked at me with a confused stare as in to say: What are you talking about?

A crewmate suggested voting for me and to put me in the time-out capsule. This was a set up wasn't it... Dark blue looked at me with sad eyes as he couldn't do anything, the innocent people who were blamed looked at me like the villain. It is game over...

The only sound I heard from Oranges side was him sneezing, turns out he can make a sound after all... his brother gave him a handkerchief to clean up... It was the same one.

Meeting

It looked exactly like the handkerchief I found in the vents. It finally clicked, no wonder he wanted to me call the meeting. He was the impostor, and I was blamed for it. He had played it perfectly and I had been outplayed. I was lost and betrayed… where is Green when I need him. While I was being taken to the time-out capsule Green screamed. Where did you even come from?

"Get your hands off my friend!" he shouted. I turned around with tears in my eyes. He was holding a handkerchief just like that... I have never met a man more impressive than Green.

Green never was slow; I just took him for one as I never thought about what was going on in his head. He was just different and that is okay. He was late to the meeting as he had to try and retrieve that handkerchief from the vent. I don't know how he did it. But I am glad he did.

He had put sprinkled some spices where Orange was to make him sneeze to check whether he had a handkerchief.

.

It turns out he was my sensei all along, it took a

while to convince the others, but Dark blue helped Green and with his charisma they proved their point after all. I have never seen a more shocked face than Pinks. Orange was put in the time-out capsule and we should be able to enjoy our peace.

time-out capsule

Thank you, Green, you are truly my friend.

P.S. Now that Orange is in the capsule, I am taking all of his snacks. Sucks to be you Orange.

Recommendation

Visit our Author Page on Amazon For More Amazing Among us Books.

How To Draw
AMONG US CHARACTERS
Step By Step Drawing Guide

Made in the USA
Las Vegas, NV
12 May 2021